CHESS FOR KIDS

MY FIRST BOOK TO LEARN HOW TO PLAY CHESS

YURI BORISOV

INDEX

Chess is a fantastic game to learn because:

It encourages people to be creative and imaginative:

By looking at different possible plays, a scientific study has shown that both sides of the brain work together. These results were true for both professional and amateur players.

When thinking about possible moves, it's not enough to just follow patterns or play the same way you did before. You also need to look at the current options and try to imagine what could happen until the end of the game.

Teach kids that their decisions have consequences

Chess has many benefits for people of all ages, and there are some benefits that are especially good for kids. One is that it helps them understand the rules and take responsibility for what they do.

This is a sport where luck doesn't matter. Everything is out in the open, and the only thing that controls what happens next is how the players move. There is nothing apart from the game that could change how it goes.

It's fun to do and makes you feel better

One should not miss that chess continues to be a game, so it has all the good things that other games have.

It's fun and lets you talk to other participants, no regardless of how old or country they are. Players could really as well play from far away by using one of the many websites that let you do so. Also it's free " nearly free. All you need is a board and pieces or a way to connect to the internet.

It helps to learn to read better

Lastly, one of the best things about chess is that it helps kids get better at reading. A scientific investigation discovered that pupils who played chess increased their reading ability much more than students who didn't take part in any chess programs.

CHESS PIECES

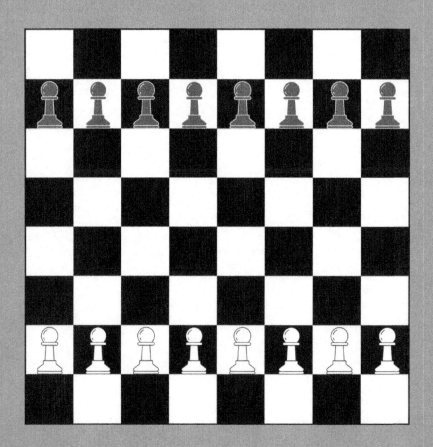

PAWN

- Every player has eight pawns
- The second row is where they go
- As you can see in the picture, they are all along the second row

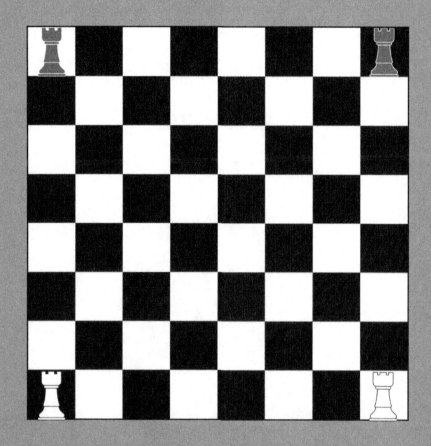

ROOK

- Everyone has two rooks
- One goes in each corner of the first row, as shown in the picture

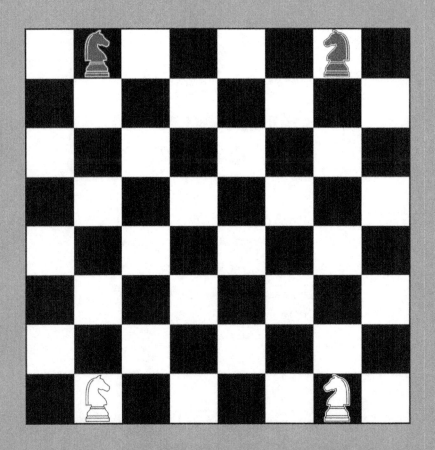

KNIGHT

- **Everyone has 2 knights**
- **Both knights are placed between the rook and the bishop.**

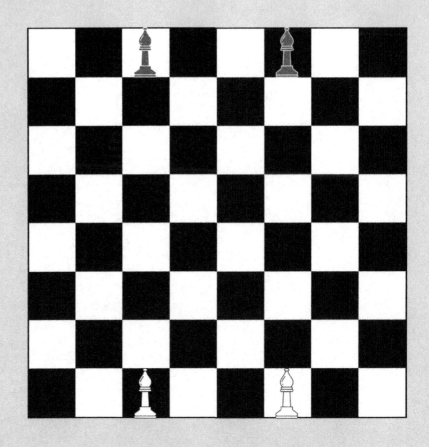

BISHOP

- Everyone has 2 bishops
- They are placed between the knight and the queen and the other between the knight and the king

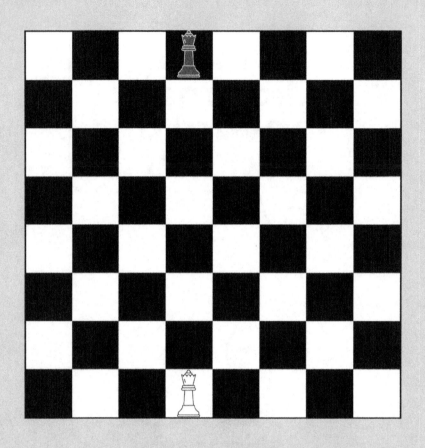

QUEEN

- Everyone has 1 queen

- It is placed between the king and the bishop

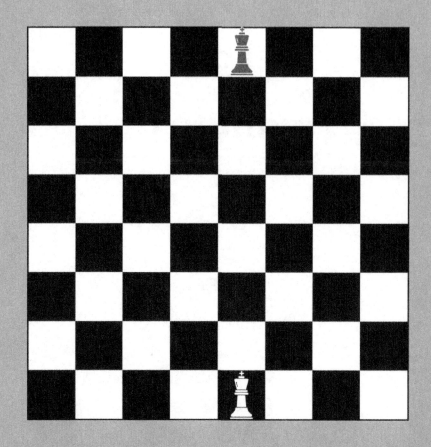

KING

- **Each player has 1 king**
- **The king is placed between the bishop and the queen**

CHESS
ELEMENTS

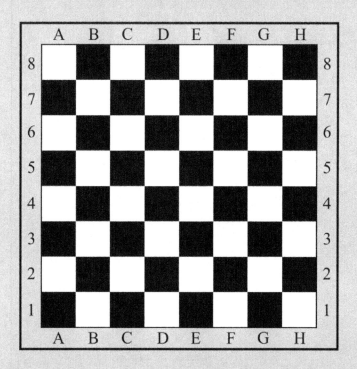

There are **64** white and **64** black squares on the board.

Each square can be found by its number and letter.

"Algebraic notation" is the name for the places where each square is.

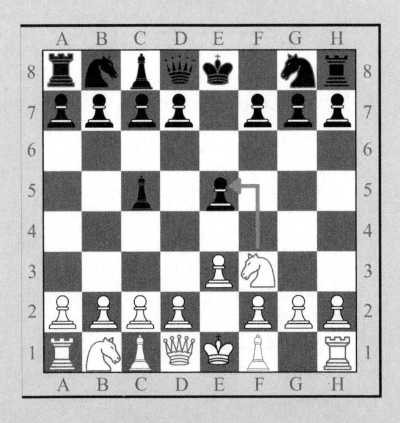

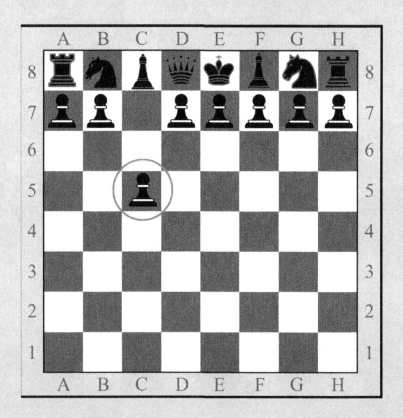

Could you tell me in which algebraic position is the pawn surrounded by a circle?

MOVEMENTS OF THE PIECES

PAWN

- Dots show which moves are possible based on where each piece is
- One square at a time, it moves forward
- It can move up to two squares forward on its first move
- It can't move in reverse
- As you can see in the picture, it can take an opponent's piece if it is on a diagonal square in front of the pawn. The black pawn piece could be caught by the white pawn. It can't move to an empty diagonal square
- It has two moves that are unique to it: promotion and "en passant"

ROOK

- Dots show what moves a rook can make from where it is right now
- You can move it across the board as much as you want
- Only one way at a time is possible
- It can only move horizontally or vertically in rows

KNIGHT

- Dots show the possible moves which a knight can make from its current position.
- It moves like an "L", 2 horizontal or vertical squares and one perpendicular square to the front or the back.
- The move ends on a different color than the one at the beginning.
- It can jump on top of whichever piece (your own or your rivals) in order to finish its move.
- You can capture a piece if it is placed on the last square where the knight goes.

BISHOP

- The dots show what moves a bishop can make from where it is at the moment
- It always moves diagonally landing on squares of the same color. A white bishop will only use the white squares and a black bishop the black squares
- In a turn, it can move as many squares as you want
- In each turn, you can only move once

QUEEN

- Dots show the possible moves which a queen can make from its current position
- It can move horizontal, vertical and diagonally, but only one direction at a time per turn
- It can move as many squares as you like at a time

KING

- Dots show the different moves a king can make from where it is now
- It can go anywhere, but only one square at a time
- It can't take a piece if another piece is there to protect it
- Its special move is called "castling," and the king moves to the side of the rook if the rook is empty and not threatened by the opponent
- One king cannot checkmate another

A FEW RULES

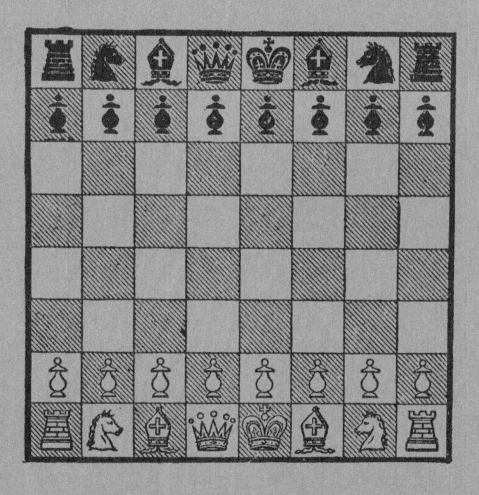

- If one of your pieces is already in a square, another one of our pieces can't go there. We can only move into a square where our opponent already has a piece. This is called "capturing or taking" the piece.

- Only one piece can move at a time for each player. The "castling" move is different.

- The player whose pieces are white moves first.
- The knight is the only piece that can jump over other pieces.

- You can't capture the king. If the king could be captured on the next turn, this is called a "check," and the king at risk must protect itself on its next move or be protected by another piece. If this isn't possible, it's checkmate, and the person whose king is in danger of being taken loses the game.

- Pawns are the only pieces that can't move backwards.
- When it is a player's turn, they must move a piece.

SPECIAL MOVEMENTS

CASTLING

is the name given to the movement when the king and the rook move at the same time.

Castling can only be used if:

- Both the king and the rook have not been moved before in this game.

- Between the king and the rook, there is no piece.

- Your king is not in check position.

- At the end of the move, the king is not on a square where an opponent's piece is threatening it.

Short castling

The king moves 2 squares to the right and the right rook moves 2 squares to the left as you can see shown on the picture.

Long castling

As you can see in the picture, the left rook moves 3 squares to the right and the king moves 2 squares to the left.

EN PASSANT

If a pawn moves two squares forward on its first move and ends up next to an opponent's pawn, the opponent's pawn can capture it as if it had moved only one square. The pawn of the winner would have to go on the diagonal square.

This move can only be made after the pawn has moved two squares forward.

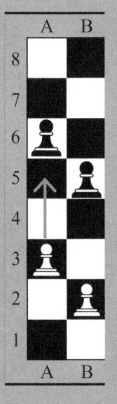

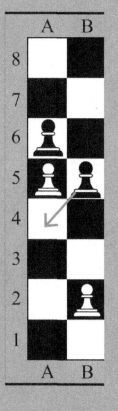

PROMOTION

If the pawn moves to the other end of the board, it can be upgraded to a better piece with more value.

Congrats!!

CHECK

Check means that a player's king is threatened and it could be taken by an opponent's piece on the next turn.

If the king piece has nowhere to go, the game is over (called "Checkmate").

Some ways to get out of a "Check" are as follows:

- Move the king to a square that is not in danger.
- Get the piece that could hurt the king.
- Stop the check by putting another piece between it and the check.

Ways to escape from check

Checkmate situation

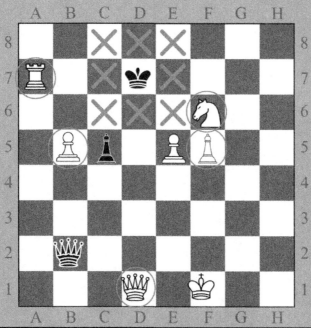

GAME OVER

1. Game over

If a player's king is in check and he can't make a move to get it out of check, the king is in checkmate and the game is over. Unlike the other pieces, the king can't be taken or move out of the game because "checkmate" ends the game.

2. Giving up on the game

Any player can quit at any time, which makes the other player the winner.

3. Tie or draw

The game can end in a draw or a tie if any of the following happen:

- The situation is called "drowned king" if neither king is in check and neither player has a move for the next turn.

- If the way the remaining pieces are set up means that neither player can get to a position where the other player has lost. For example: king vs king, king vs king and bishop, king vs king and knight, king and bishop vs king and bishop.

- If everyone agrees to draw.

d) Time wasted

If the game is played with a time limit, it could end when one of the players runs out of time. On a certain term, players can have a certain amount of time or a certain number of moves they can make.

SICILIAN DEFENSE

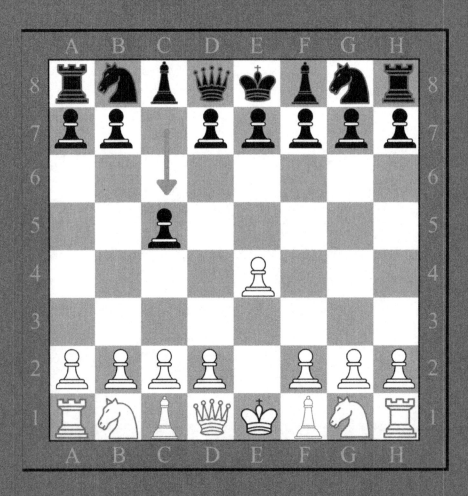

The best move for brave players with the black pieces is usually the Sicilian Defense.

It's very simple. If white moves the pawn from e2 to e4 on the first move, black could move the pawn from c7 to c5.

Most of the time, the first move for white in chess is for the pawn to go to e4, then the knight to f3, and then the pawn to d4. This is done to get the space in the middle of the board.

So, if blacks' first move after e4 is to put the pawn on c5, everything changes, and whites will have to change their strategy because they will have to move another piece.

ITALIAN GAME

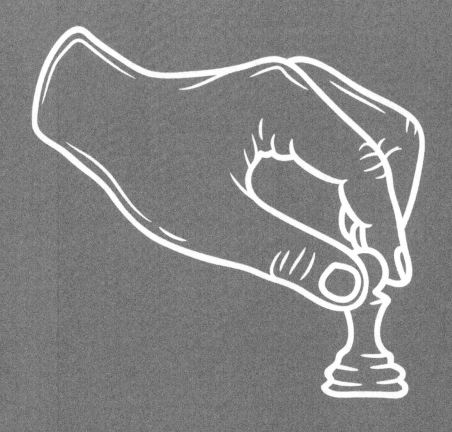

The Italian game is played by moving the e2 pawn to make room for the queen and bishop.

Steps:

- Move the pawn on e2 forward two squares. Move e7 if you are Black.
- Put the knight on square f3 (the next possible move for the knight is to trap the black pawn e5). If you are Black, move the knight to square c6 (if a piece traps the e5 pawn, your knight would trap it on the next move).
- Move your bishop to c4 to attack.

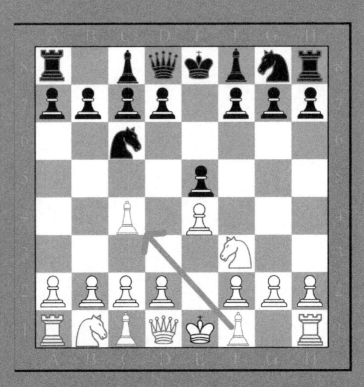

Whites or blacks can do these three steps, and they don't depend on what your opponent does. Don't forget that you're doing this to make space for the bishop and queen.

After this, you can do a number of things, such as:

- Keep your king safe: think about your next move (this move is explained on chapter 2)
- The white bishop makes it possible for a black piece to move up, but you would have to take the f7 pawn first. You might be able to catch the f7 pawn by moving the Knight on f3 twice.

Depending on what the other player does, you can do whatever you want. Stay calm and think about your next three steps at all times.

SLAV
DEFENSE

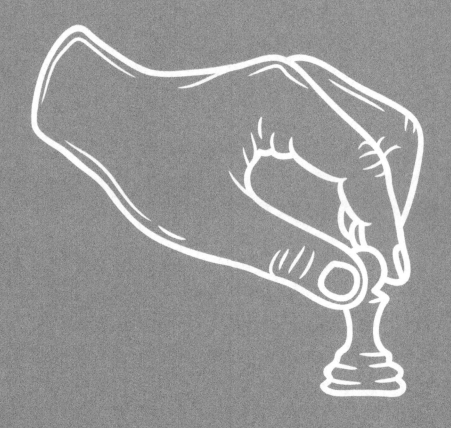

The Slav Defense is a way for black to protect the pawn on d5 with the pawn on c7.

This is a common response to the Queen's Gambit, which is when white moves their pawns to the d4 and c4 squares.

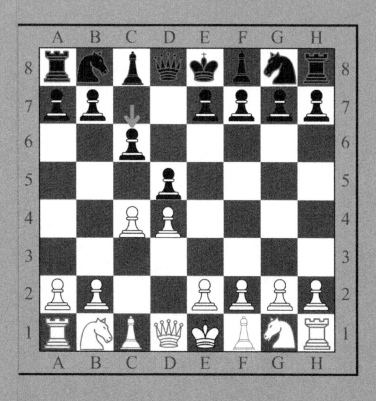

The Slav Defense is a way to start a game that was made popular by great Slavic players. It is a response to the Queen's Gambit move that is very popular right now.

In this defense you will build a wall that blacks can't get through and that whites won't be able to break down.

After that, you could move the pawn on e7 up to e6 to make a chain of pawns. Be aware that if you do these moves, your c8 Bishop will be trapped.

FRENCH DEFENSE

Every chess player should learn the French Defense as one of their first opening moves.

If you're Black and White's first move is e4, you could move your pawn from e7 to e6 as your first move.

If you are playing as blacks, then you could move your d7 pawn to d5 on your second move because they would already be safe enough to advance.

If whites takes tour d5 pawn, your d6 pawn will be ready to take that piece on the next turn.

If you play this opening as blacks, you should know that it will be more difficult to move your bishop from c8.

For now, that's all...

Did you enjoyplease leave me a review on the website where you bought it. It will only take a minute, and it would mean the world to me.

I really appreciate that you took the time to read this book and write a review.

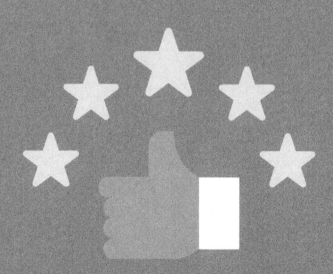

Best of luck
in your fights!!

Printed in Great Britain
by Amazon